GW01605762

Tony Hickey

THE MATCHLESS MICE

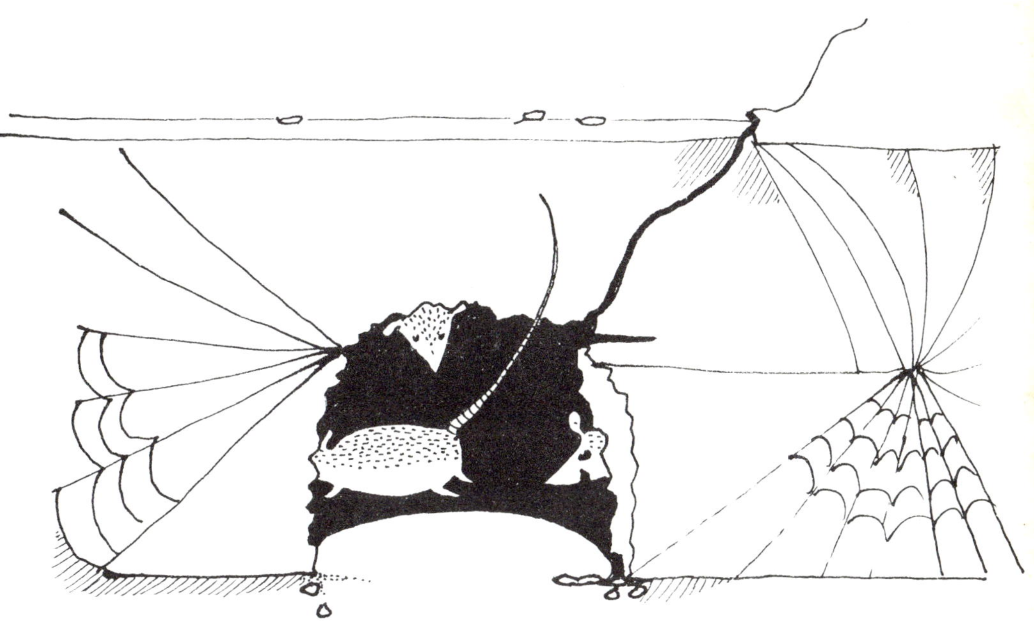

Illustrated by Pauline Bewick

GERALDINE PRESS

First published in 1979 by
The Geraldine Press
90 Lower Baggot Street, Dublin 2

ISBN 0 900068 45 0

Printed in Ireland by
Cahill Printers Limited

CONTENTS

1

Before the Quarrel

The Matchless Mice lived behind the skirting board next to the fireplace of the old drawingroom of Mangold Mansion.

I call it 'the old drawingroom' because it was a long time since any people had lived in the house.

Indeed it was a long time since any people had even been near the house.

You could almost say that Mangold Mansion had been forgotten. This can happen to houses that have been empty for a long time. It can happen even more easily to houses that are large and dark and rather lonely looking.

Mangold Mansion was like that; large and dark, and rather lonely looking.

It hadn't always been like that of course. Once it had been a fine, big, bright house, full of happy people.

It had had a lovely garden with a high wall around it. Beyond this wall, green fields had stretched as far as the eye could see to the edge of the city.

Then the city had started to grow. It spread further and further towards Mangold Mansion.

The green fields were sold. New houses were built on them.

Then the people who owned Mangold Mansion moved away. Soon the grass in the garden grew long and tangled. Flowers and rose bushes went wild. Tall weeds grew everywhere. Trees and shrubs became enormous. Thick ivy covered the garden wall.

A few slates fell off the roof. A few windows were blown in by winter storms.

It became very hard to imagine that Mangold Mansion had ever been a lovely place in which to live.

Indeed the few people who still remembered how it had once been said that Mangold Mansion was now haunted.

This, of course, was not true.

But the Matchless Mice and all the other mice who lived in the Mansion were delighted that no humans ever came near the place.

Grandfather Matchless used say, "I don't give a baked bean if no human ever sets foot in Mangold Mansion again. Country people would be bad enough, but city people!" He would sigh and shake his head. "I wouldn't ask the wildest water rat to live in the same house as city folk."

The other mice would nod their heads in agreement. They knew that Grandfather Matchless was right.

Yet even if he had not been right, very few of the other mice who lived in Mangold Mansion would have dared to argue with him.

There were two reasons for this.

The first reason was that Grandfather Matchless was the oldest mouse in Mangold Mansion. He said this meant he was also the wisest mouse in the Mansion.

The second reason few mice would argue with Grandfather Matchless was because he always insisted on being right, even when it was as plain as the whiskers on his face that he was wrong.

Grandfather Matchless was also a very proud mouse. He claimed that his family had lived longer in Mangold Mansion than any other mouse family.

He would say, very proudly, to any mouse who would listen, "The Matchless Mice family have been living in Mangold Mansion for well over five hundred years. That is why we have the name 'Matchless'. It means there has never been our equal or 'match' among mice when it comes to living so long in the one place. That is also of course why we live in the drawingroom. Being the most important family in the Mansion, we have, of course, the finest room."

Now Grandfather Matchless forgot one very important thing. It was this.

If anyone, mouse or human, goes on saying the same thing over and over again, it can be very boring to listen to.

But if what the mouse, or human, keeps saying over and over again is how important he and his family are, then, sooner or later, those who have to listen are not only going to become very fed-up. They are also going to become very cross.

This is exactly how the quarrel began.

2

The Quarrel

It was a fine summer morning. Grandfather Matchless was lying in the long grass, enjoying a pipe of nettle tobacco.

The sun was so warm, the grass was so green, the sky was so blue, that Grandfather Matchless felt very happy. He also felt like talking.

A group of young mice passed by.

Grandfather Matchless called out to them.

They hurried over to him, delighted to be noticed by so important a mouse.

He patted the ground.

The young mice sat in a circle around him.

"Well now," said Grandfather Matchless, puffing slowly on his pipe. "I'm sure you would all like me to tell you the story of how the Matchless Mice have lived in Mangold Mansion for over five hundred years."

"Oh yes, we'd love to hear that," the young mice said eagerly.

"Well I wouldn't," a much older voice said crossly.

The long grass beside Grandfather Matchless parted.

There, in a small clearing that Grandfather had not noticed, stood old Crumbs Kitchen. He was only slightly younger than Grandfather Matchless.

Yet, he and Grandfather Matchless had never been good friends.

Now they glared at each other like two enemies.

"What did you just say?" Grandfather Matchless asked. "It *was* you who spoke just now?"

"You know well it was me who spoke," snapped old Crumbs. "Just as you know perfectly well what I said."

"I'm afraid you are mistaken," Grandfather said, as grandly as he could. "I haven't the slightest idea what you were trying to say."

"Then, I'll say it again," old Crumbs declared. "I, and many of the other mice in Mangold Mansion, are sick to death listenin' to you and your old GUFF."

Grandfather Matchless could hardly believe his ears. "GUFF?" he said. "What exactly do you mean by Guff?"

"You know perfectly well what I mean," old Crumbs declared. "I mean all the old guff, all the old nonsense, you are always goin' on about how your family have lived in Mangold Mansion for five hundred years. Well, that is impossible."

"And how would you know what was possible or impossible?" Grandfather Matchless smiled nastily as he spoke. "You, whose ancestors arrived here in an empty sardine tine during the great flood of 1929?"

The tone of voice and the smile used by Grandfather Matchless put old Crumbs into a blazing temper.

He drew himself up to his full two inches of height. "I'll tell you how I know it is impossible for the family of the Matchless Mice to have lived here for five hundred years," he said. "It is impossible because Mangold Mansion was not built until 1900. Mangold Mansion is not even one hundred years old."

"Nonsense," said Grandfather Matchless.

But in spite of the way he spoke, Grandfather Matchless suddenly felt nervous.

He felt even more nervous when he looked at the circle of young mice still seated around him. They had not said a word since old Crumbs had interrupted. Yet somehow Grandfather Matchless wished that they would speak. Surely they did not believe what old Crumbs had just said?

Old Crumbs laughed. It was as though he knew that Grandfather Matchless was nervous. "Nonsense, is it?" he said. "Well next time you are up at the front door step, have a look at the date carved above the fanlight."

At last, one of the younger mice spoke in a very quiet voice. "But there is no date carved there," he said. "We'd have seen it long before this if there was."

"It's been covered with ivy, just like the garden wall has been, for years and years," old Crumbs explained. "Well the ivy fell off last night. Now the date that the house was built is there for all to see. And the date is 1900! The Matchless Mice couldn't have lived here for five hundred years."

"But what about the name 'Matchless'?" the same young mouse asked. "The Matchless Mice were named because there was never their equal for living in the same place for so long."

Old Crumbs laughed again. This time his laugh was nastier than Grandfather's smile had been. "More non-sense," he said. "In fact, the truth probably is that they were called 'Matchless' because there was never their equal for putting on airs and graces and for talking rubbish."

There was a stunned silence. All the mice, including old Crumbs, waited for Grandfather Matchless to speak.

But for the first time in his life Grandfather Matchless did not know what to say.

The news about the date above the front door had come as a great shock to him.

Yet old Crumbs would hardly have made up a story like that. It was too easy to check if it was true.

Yet if it was true, what then?

It would mean that the Matchless Mice were not really special.

It would mean that the Matchless Mice were just common or garden house-mice. Grandfather Matchless needed time to think. He needed to be alone.

Grandfather Matchless stared at the circle of the young mice.

He would have to do something, but something clever.

Then he had a brilliant idea.

He would pretend that old Crumbs Kitchen was not worth even noticing.

He gave a little yawn.

He put his pipe down on a large flat stone where it

could do no harm.

He stretched, glanced up at the sky, yawned again. Then slowly, very slowly he allowed his eyes to close.

In a few seconds he seemed to be fast asleep.

The silence lasted a few more seconds.

Then Grandfather heard gentle scuffling noises.

"That," he said to himself, "is the others creeping quietly away."

All the same, just to be safe, he waited a few minutes longer before opening his eyes.

When he did open them, he saw to his annoyance that, while the circle of young mice had vanished, old Crumbs was still standing there, glaring at him.

Old Crumbs snorted, "Oh yes, oh yes," he said. "Very clever. Pretending to be asleep. Pretending not to care. Pretending to be too GRAND to be upset. But what I said is true. One-hundred-per-cent true."

When old Crumbs said, "one-hundred-per-cent true," his voice squeaked like an old tin box being opened.

But still Grandfather did not look at him.

Instead Grandfather Matchless just picked up his pipe, stretched himself slightly and gazed up at the blue, blue sky.

This made old Crumbs even more cross. In fact he completely lost his temper.

His fur turned bright pink. His eyes bulged. He jumped up and down in the long grass. He shouted a great number of very spiteful things about the Matchless Mice.

Soon almost every mouse in the house knew there was a terrible quarrel going on in the garden.

Many of them left their work and hurried out to see

who on earth old Crumbs could be shouting at.

When they got as far as the front door step, they saw a circle of young mice, standing very still and gazing up at the fanlight above the door.

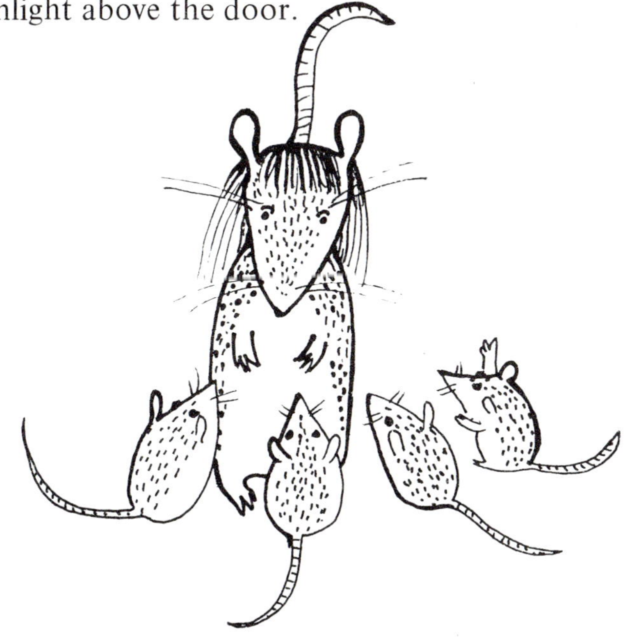

These were the same circle of young mice who had been in the garden when the quarrel began.

The young mice looked so serious that the other mice stopped and said, "What's wrong? What's happening?"

"It's the date," the young mice said.

"Date? What date?" demanded Alta Attic, who lived at the very top of the Mansion.

"The date the house was built. 1900," the young mice said. "It means that what Grandfather Matchless has been saying can't be true. The Matchless Mice can't have lived here for five hundred years. Old Crumbs Kitchen discovered the truth. It's he you can hear quarrelling with Grandfather Matchless out in the long grass."

"Grandfather Matchless doesn't seem to be saying very much then," remarked Alta Attic.

"Maybe that's because there is nothing he CAN say," Polly Pantry said. "After all, there is the date for all to see. Maybe if we had not been so busy agreeing with Grandfather Matchless, we would have noticed it long ago."

"That is true," some other mouse said. "After all what do we know about the Matchless Mice except what Grandfather Matchless has told us?"

At that very moment old Crumbs pushed his way out of the long grass.

He was still in a temper. He still shook and quivered. But he was no longer shouting. Instead he muttered away to himself under his breath.

When he saw the great crowd of mice waiting on the front door step, he stopped.

Suddenly he realised what a serious thing he had done.

Suddenly he realised that many of the mice were looking at him the way they had once looked at Grandfather Matchless.

Suddenly he knew that he was expected to be the leader of the Mangold Mansion mice.

He was not sure if he liked this idea.

He was not sure if he wanted to be bothered with other mice's problems.

Before a word could be said to him, old Crumbs rushed around the side of the Mansion.

The back door was open.

In a flash, he was safely in the great gloomy kitchen where he lived with Mrs. Crumbs.

3

After the Quarrel

Mrs. Crumbs Kitchen was deaf. This meant that she had not heard a word her husband had said in the garden. Neither had she heard the noise the mice had made on the front door step.

All the same when she looked at old Crumbs she knew something was wrong.

"What have you been up to then?" she demanded. "And don't say 'nothing' because I know that you have."

"Well there was a bit of a quarrel," old Crumbs said.

"A quarrel?" said Mrs. Crumbs. "Who with?"

"Grandfather Matchless," old Crumbs said, suddenly feeling ashamed of the way he had behaved.

Mrs. Crumbs sighed. She said, "Honestly, Crumbs, a mouse of your age should have more sense. I suppose you made a right exhibition of yourself."

Old Crumbs knew that what Mrs. Crumbs said was true. He had made an exhibition of himself. He should have tried to stay calm and dignified like Grandfather.

But it was too late now. He had said what he had said in the way he had said it.

Anyway he had only spoken the truth.

Suddenly old Crumbs no longer felt ashamed.

He said angrily, "Maybe I ought to have just sat there in the long grass and had my day ruined by Grandfather Matchless. Maybe I should have let him make mincemeat

of me. The whole house knows the truth about him now."

And indeed the whole house did by now know what old Crumbs had said. Even Grandfather Matchless's own family, who had paid no attention to the sound of old Crumbs shouting in the garden, knew.

Alta Attic had called in on her way back upstairs to tell Grandmother Matchless what had happened.

Grandmother Matchless just smiled when she heard about the date over the door. "I am quite sure old Crumbs Kitchen had got it all wrong," she said.

All the same when Alta Attic had finally left the drawing room, Grandmother Matchless and the rest of the Matchless Mice hurried out into the garden to find Grandfather.

He was still sitting in the long grass, smoking his pipe of nettle tobacco.

He looked happy enough.

But his family realised from the way that his paw shook, when he took his pipe out of his mouth, that he was very upset.

Grandmother Matchless said, "Pay no attention to what old Crumbs said. He's jealous of you."

Moaner, his eldest mouse-son, said, "The date over the door doesn't prove a single thing."

Scratch, his little grand-mouse, said, "The date over the door might be the year that the DOOR was built. The house must have been built long before they put up the front door."

Flap, Scratch's mother, thought Scratch was very clever to have thought of that.

But Grandfather Matchless just smiled and said, "Isn't

it a lovely day? Oh what a lovely day it is."

Then he closed his eyes again.

It was as though the quarrel had never happened. It was as though there was no such mouse as old Crumbs Kitchen.

Later that day, Grandfather Matchless met old Crumbs in the hall of Mangold Mansion.

Grandfather walked straight past him. He did not even seem to see his enemy.

But this did not annoy old Crumbs.

Old Crumbs was too happy now to be annoyed.

Ever since the quarrel in the garden, old Crumbs found that he had lots of new friends.

Everywhere he went, mice stopped to talk to him.

Several mice began to call him "Mouse Kitchen" instead of just "Old Crumbs".

He felt as though he was the king of Mangold Mansion.

Mrs. Crumbs Kitchen was delighted to see old Crumbs so happy.

All the same she had some advice for him.

"Don't be too sure of yourself," she said. "Grandfather Matchless will not give in that easily. If you ask me, he is at this very moment sitting out there in the long grass, planning his revenge on you."

Old Crumbs thought for a few seconds about what Mrs. Crumbs had said.

Then he nodded his head. "You're right," he said. "I think I'll go and see what the old Joker is up to."

4

Grandfather Matchless gets a letter

Old Crumbs ran quickly through the long grass to where Grandfather Matchless was sitting, half-dozing in the bright sunshine.

Everything looked and sounded normal.

Then there was an unexpected noise overhead; a gentle, whirring, silky noise.

Old Crumbs looked up.

There, hovering above the long grass, was the Butterfly Post.

For a second old Crumbs thought the Butterfly Post was just resting. Then he realised that there was another sound apart from the whirring of its wings. The Butterfly Post was calling out in a soft breathless kind of way, "Grandfather Matchless . . . Grandfather Matchless, wake up, wake up."

But Grandfather Matchless gave no indication of having heard.

The Butterfly Post came close enough to Grandfather for its wings to brush very slightly against Grandfather's nose.

"Wha . . wha . . what . . what's that?" Grandfather asked sleepily. Then he gave a loud sneeze, and rubbed at his nose and opened his eyes; all at the same time. "What's happened?"

"I have a letter for you," the Butterfly Post said.

"A letter?" Grandfather Matchless was amazed. The

mice that lived in Mangold Mansion had very little to do with the outside world.

Old Crumbs stepped forward to where he could be seen. He threw back his head scornfully and said, "Oh writing letters to himself now; that's his latest way to try and seem important."

But old Crumbs was wrong. There really was a letter for Grandfather. But Grandfather, as soon as he saw his enemy old Crumbs, thought that a trick was being played on him. He changed his tone of voice from one of surprise to one of scorn. "A letter indeed, Mr. Butterfly Post. Maybe you would do me the favour of reading this letter. The sun is so bright I would never be able to see the words."

"Well, I don't know, I'm sure," the Butterfly Post said to himself. "Now I have to read letters to mice." But then he thought, "Say nothing. Soonest started, soonest ended."

He opened the letter and read, "Dear Grandfather Matchless, For quite some time now I've been meaning to come and visit you and yours. Now at last I find I can manage it. I'll arrive at Mangold Mansion as soon as I can. Your ever loving nephew, Michael Mouse Matchless-Chedderington,in Manchester."

Grandfather Matchless went as pale as an uncooked pancake. "Is this someone's idea of a joke?" he demanded.

The Butterfly Post glared, in so much as a Butterfly Post can be said to glare. Then he snapped, in so much as Butterfly Post can ever be said to snap. Then he said, "Do you think I've nothing better to do than fly around in this warm weather delivering jokes?"

"I . . . I'm sorry, I meant no harm." Grandfather Matchless raised a trembling paw by way of apology. Then, turning quickly, he staggered, rather than ran, back to the house.

Grandmother Matchless was waiting for him at the door of the drawingroom. "What is it?" she asked. "What's wrong?"

Grandfather Matchless stared at her with great frightened eyes. "Inside," he said, "go along inside."

When they were safely in their own dwelling, Grandfather said, "You'll never guess what's happened."

"I'm not sure I want to guess what's happened," Grandmother Matchless replied. "I'd much sooner you told me."

"I've received a letter. A . . a . . ." Grandfather's voice shook and trembled. He found it impossible to continue. He held out the letter to Grandmother.

Quickly she read it. When she had finished, she too had turned pale. She collapsed, rather than sat, onto a chair.

"You know then who this Michael Mouse Matchless Chedderington is then?" Grandfather asked.

Grandmother nodded. "It must be the son of You-Know-Who . . ."

"Exactly," said Grandfather, "exactly. If old Crumbs Kitchen could use something silly like the date over the front door to harm us, think of what he will manage when You-Know-Who's son arrives."

And Grandfather Matchless was right.

'You-Know-Who' was the way that Grandfather and Grandmother always spoke of Grandfather's youngest brother, Ashes. Ashes had joined a gang of field mice, and had been sent away from home.

The story of his disgrace had been kept from the other mice in Mangold Mansion.

Indeed Ashes's name had never even been mentioned to Moaner or Flap or little Scratch. And now, just as old Crumbs Kitchen was doing his best to ruin the good name of the Matchless Mice, the son of the black sheep, or maybe I should say 'black mouse', of the family was coming for a visit.

"Ruined," declared Grandfather. "That is what we are. Totally ruined."

Grandmother said, "You will just have to write to him. Tell him that it's not convenient right now for us to have visitors."

"How can I write when there's no address on the letter?" replied Grandfather. "Besides he has probably left Manchester already."

Just then, little Scratch came hurrying in. "There's a very strange-looking mouse outside," he said, "and I think he is looking for you."

Grandfather groaned. "He's here. He's here already," groaned Grandfather. "Go out and bring him in before anyone sees him."

But the strange mouse was already standing at the entrance to the Matchless Mice's dwelling.

5

The Visitors Arrive

The strange-looking mouse wore a lovely tweed jacket. On his head he had a white knitted hat with a tassel at the back.

Over his shoulder, he carried a bundle on a stick.

By the look of him, he had travelled a long way down long dusty roads.

He stared at Grandfather Matchless.

"An tusa dearthấir mo sheanathar?" he asked Grandfather.

"What?" said Grandfather in amazement.

The strange-looking mouse repeated the question. "An tusa dearthấir mo sheanathar?"

"Well, by the hokey," said Grandfather Matchless. "I've heard some strange stories of the odd way they speak in England. But the way this mouse speaks takes the biscuit altogther."

Little Scratch roared with laughter. "It's not English that he's speaking," he said. "It's Irish."

Grandfather stared at Scratch. "And what would a mouse from Manchester be doing speaking Irish?" he demanded.

"I don't think he is from England," said Grandmother Matchless. "He doesn't look like an English mouse to me. Oh, if only Flap was here!"

Flap had grown up in a house owned by a schoolteacher. She managed to learn quite a lot of Irish by listening to him and his family.

But of course Flap was nowhere to be seen.

"Never here when she's wanted," Grandfather Matchless said, "Never."

Little Scratch said, "I'll talk to our visitor. Mother taught me Irish ages and ages ago."

Little Scratch stepped forward, gave a little bow and said to the strange-looking mouse, "Cad is ainm duit?"

"Is mise Arán MacLeasa," arsa an luch beag stróinséartha. "Agus cad as ar tháinig tú?" b'shin an dara cheist a chuir Scratch.

"O'n Lios atá in aice Baile an Bhuille siar ón Sliabh Mór," arsa'n luch beag stróinséartha.

"What's he saying? What's he saying?" demanded Grandfather. "Am I to be left standing here like a fool, not knowing what's been said in my own house?"

Scratch quickly explained. "He says his name is Arân MacLeasa. He has come from the Fort near the town of Buille beyond the great mountain."

"And what does he want here?" Grandfather asked.

Scratch asked Aran why he has come to Mangold Mansion.

"Tá mé ag lorg dearthair mo sheanathar," arsa Aran.

Scratch turned to Grandfather, "He says he is looking for his grandfather's brother."

"Well tell him he's made a mistake," Grandfather said. "Tell him to try the other floors. Tell him we have visitors coming."

But Arán shook his head when Scratch told him this. "Tá mé sa seomra ceart," ar seisean. "Nach é seo an parlús – parlús an Mangold Mansion? Dúirt siad liom sa bhaile gur annseo a bheadh an chlann."

Scratch, why by now felt he was watching a football match from having to turn from Arán to Grandfather, told Grandfather what Arán had said. "Arán says he is sure he is in the right room. They told him at the Fort that he would find his relatives in the drawingroom of Mangold Mansion."

"I don't care what they told him," Grandfather said. Then he stopped. Arán had taken the bundle off his shoulder and placed it on the ground.

Very carefully Arán unwrapped the bundle. He took out a sheet of old yellow paper.

He opened the paper and held it out.

There was a drawing of a mouse on the sheet of paper.

"Sin é deartháir mo sheanathar," ar seisean.

Grandfather Matchless and Grandmother Matchless stared at the drawing. Their mouths fell open in amazement.

"Do you recognise the mouse in the drawing?" little Scratch asked nervously.

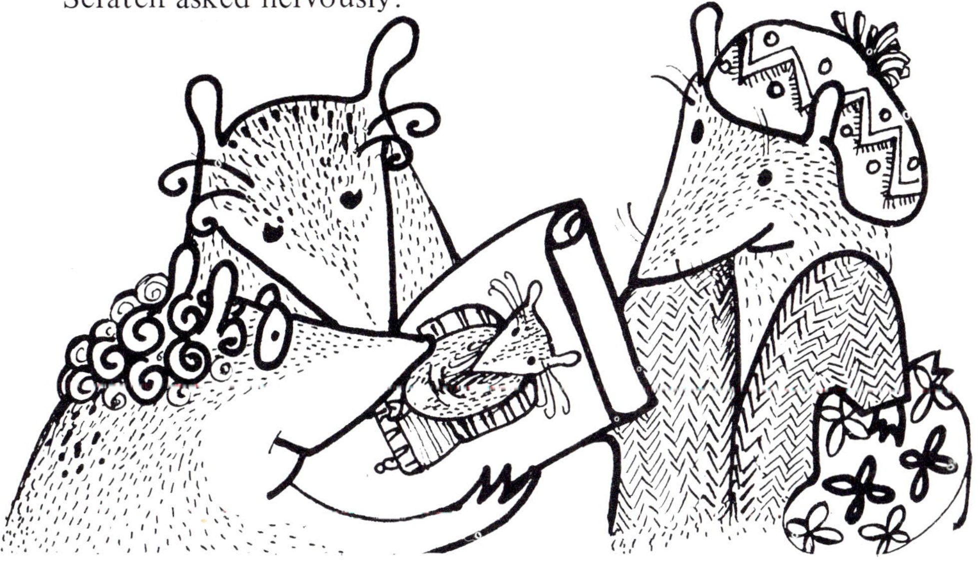

Grandfather managed to speak. "Yes," he said very slowly. "I recognise the mouse in the drawing. It is a picture of my own father."

"Then Arán has the right room," little Scratch said.

"Yes," said Grandfather. "Only it is not the brother of his grandfather that he is looking for. It is MY FATHER he wants."

"That could be the same thing," said Grandmother.

But that was all she was allowed to say.

Grandfather Matchless held up his paw for silence.

"Ask our visitor the reason for his visit," Grandfather Matchless said to little Scratch.

Scratch did as he was told.

Arán spoke very softly and very quickly.

When he has finished, it was Scratch's turn to stand with his mouth open.

"Well," demanded Grandfather Matchless impatiently. "What did he say?"

Scratch gave a little cough before speaking. "Well," he said. "Well, you see . . . It's . . . it's like this . . .?"

"Like what? Like what?" Grandfather Matchless almost shouted. "Like what?"

"Well, well, Arán says he has been sent here by his branch of the family to tell our branch of the family that all is forgiven."

"Forgiven? All what is forgiven?" Grandfather Matchless's voice was suddenly very weak.

"All the trouble or as Arán calls it 'An trioblóid'. It seems that there was some kind of quarrel between your father and his father. That was why your father left home to come and live here in Mangold Mansion."

"What?" said Grandfather. "Is this mouse trying to

tell me that our family have only lived here since my father's time? Is he trying to say that our name is not even 'Matchless'? Is he trying to say that my father was the black mouse of his family?"

An even worse thought came into Grandfather's mind. His voice became little more than a whisper. "Is he trying to say that my father was no better than 'You-Know-Who'?"

Just then they all heard a sound outside the door of the drawingroom.

Quick as a flash, Grandfather rushed towards the door. "Of course, of course," he said. "Now I know. Now I know. It's a trick. Old Crumbs Kitchen sent this mouse up here to try and frighten me with his story. Not a word of it is true." He gave a loud laugh. "And old Crumbs is now standing outside listening to all that's been said."

But when Grandfather Matchless got to the door of the drawingroom, it was not old Crumbs Kitchen he saw.

Instead, standing in a pool of bright sunlight, was a real city-slicker of a mouse. He wore a dark grey suit with a flower in the buttonhole. He had a bowler hat on his head. In his hand, he carried a walking stick.

He gave a big grin when he saw Grandfather Matchless.

Then he held out his paw and, in a voice that sounded like rain on a tin roof, said, "Uncle Tealeaf? Are you Uncle Tealeaf? But of course you are Uncle Tealeaf."

Grandfather Matchless suddenly felt as though he was going mad.

The city mouse stared at Grandfather. "Didn't you get my letter?" he asked. "Don't you recognise me?

They say I am very like my father. I am the son of your brother, Ashes. I am Michael Mouse Matchless-Chedderington, all the way from Manchester, come to see the family mansion."

There was a pause.

Then Michael said, "But of course you could not have received my letter. Otherwise I would be able to smell it."

"Smell it? Smell WHAT?" Grandfather asked. He was suddenly feeling weak again.

"Why the cake of course," Michael said. "Dad told me that whenever there was a special occasion at Mangold Mansion that the Matchless Mice baked a cake."

Michael stared at Grandfather Matchless. "I say," he said, "are you alright? You do seem to have gone rather pale."

And indeed Grandfather Matchless was now both weak and pale.

And who could blame him for that?

In a few hours, his world had been turned upside down. Not a word his father had told him about the Matchless Mice family was true.

Now here was the son of his own good-for-nothing brother, standing on the landing of Mangold Mansion.

While inside was Arán, the Irish-speaking mouse.

If old Crumbs Kitchen ever found out who the visiting mice were, Grandfather Matchless could never hold up his head again.

The only thing he could do was keep the two visitors out of sight until it was time for them to return home.

But, as this thought came to him, Grandfather saw what looked like a faint shadow move in a dark corner of the stairs.

It was old Crumbs hiding there, listening to all that was being said.

"Why the SNEAK!" Grandfather said to himself.

If there was one thing Grandfather HATED, it was SNEAKS.

Well old Crumbs, the SNEAK, was not going to hear anything that would please him.

Out loud, in the happiest voice he could manage, Grandfather Matchless said, "Michael, ould son, of course we got your letter. It arrived only a few minutes ago. We haven't had time to bake the cake yet. But don't worry. We will have it ready by this evening. Come in. Come in and meet the rest of the family."

Michael, smiling happily, followed Grandfather into the drawingroom.

Standing in his dark corner, old Crumbs sniggered to himself. "Huh!" he said. "More nonsense. Bake a cake, will you, Grandfather Matchless? We will see about that. Because if I don't stop you, then maybe the NEW CAT at the Supermarket will."

And old Crumbs Kitchen went scampering down the stairs laughing merrily.

6

To the Supermarket

The sun was still shining brightly when old Crumbs got to the front door step.

The door step itself was empty.

All the mice in the house had seen the date over the door by now.

But old Crumbs Kitchen knew that there were bound to be mice out in the long grass. He would go and tell them the news about the visitors in the drawing room.

Old Crumbs was certain there was something strange going on, something that Grandfather Matchless wanted no other mouse to know about.

With a whoop and a holler, old Crumbs ran towards the long grass. He dived into it, just like you or I might dive into the sea.

He felt so pleased with himself that he rolled around in the grass for a few minutes. Then he heard a voice.

It was the voice of Moaner, Grandfather Matchless's son, talking to his wife, Flap.

Moaner said, "Why, Flap, look! There's little Scratch running down the path after his Grandfather and Grandmother."

Flap said, "Now where on earth could they be going to? And in such a hurry as well."

Old Crumbs burst out laughing.

The long grass beside him parted. Moaner and Flap looked down at him in amazement.

"It's old Crumbs Kitchen," said Moaner. "What can he be laughing at?"

"Maybe he's crying," said Flap. "Maybe he has hay fever."

The idea of a mouse having hay fever made old Crumbs laugh even more. He held his sides. "Hay fever," he managed to say. "HAY FEVER."

He rolled around some more in the grass. "You Matchless Mice will be the death of me yet. Hay fever," he shrieked.

"Baking cakes," he shrieked.

"Supermarkets," he shrieked.

"Baking cakes? Supermarkets? What do you mean, old Crumbs?" Moaner asked.

"The visitors," old Crumbs tried to speak properly. "More nonsense! Visitors! All I can say is that I hope that the foolish pride of old Grandfather Matchless is not the cause of his nearest and dearest being eaten by a cat."

"A cat? A cat? Eaten by a cat?" Flap said. Then she started to run around in a circle. She looked as though she had suddenly lost her way.

In fact that was why she was called 'Flap'. Every time anything went wrong, she would get into a terrible flap.

Moaner stared, horrified, at old Crumbs who was still shaking with laughter.

Then he grabbed Flap by the paw. Together they ran back to the house.

"That'll learn them," old Crumbs thought. "That'll learn them."

7

The Tale of the Cat

When Moaner and Flap rushed into the drawingroom and saw two strange mice there, they did not know what to think.

"Who are you?" demanded Moaner. "What are you doing here?"

"I'm Michael Mouse Matchless-Chedderington from Manchester," said Michael. "You must be my cousin Moaner."

Michael turned and pointed at Arán. "And I think this mouse here is part of the family as well."

"Conas tá tú," arsa Arán. "Tá mise agus tusa saghas gaolmhar le chéile."

"Gaolmhar?" arsa Flap.

Tháinig an chuid Gaeilge a bhí aici ón am a raibh sí ina conaí i dtigh an mhúinteora ar ais.

"Nice sound that mouse makes," said Michael. "I wish I could understand what it is he is saying."

"He's speaking Irish," Flap explained. "He says that he and Moaner are cousins."

"Oh really?" said Michael. "That means he and I are cousins as well."

But Moaner had no time to talk about being cousins. "What is all this about being eaten by a cat?" he demanded.

"Eaten by a cat?" Michael looked carefully at Moaner. "Are you feeling alright? Are you sure you

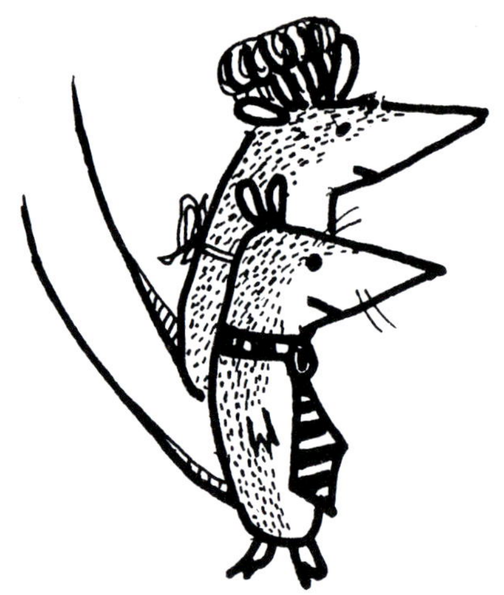

haven't been sitting too long out in the sun?"

"Of course I haven't been too long in the sun," Moaner answered. "But Flap and I met old Crumbs just now. It was he who said something about being eaten by a cat."

"Search me, old thing," said Michael. "I heard nothing about a cat."

Moaner turned to Flap. "Ask the Irish speaker what he knows."

"Ar chuala tú riamh faoin gcat?" arsa Flap.

"Níor chuala mé," arsa Arán. "An bhfuil tú ag rá go bhfuil cat sa teach seo?"

"O, ní hea, ní hea," arsa Flap. "Ach chuala Moaner agus mé féin go raibh sé sórt dainséarach don chlann."

"Tá an triúr acu imithe síos go dtí an siopa," arsa Arán.

"Go dtí an siopa!" Flap gasped. "To the shop, the shop . . . He says they've gone to the shop."

"Oh is that what all the fuss is about," said Michael. "Only they haven't gone to the shop. They've gone to the supermarket."

"I . . I . . I don't believe it," whispered Moaner.

"Oh but it is true," said Michael. "They have gone to get the things needed to bake the famous Matchless Mice cake . . ."

Michael stared at Flap and Moaner . . . "I say," he said. "You don't mean that this cat you've been talking about is down in the supermarket?"

"Yes," said Moaner.

"But surely they would know there was a cat there," said Michael.

"No," said Moaner. "The supermarket is new. There was a small shop there before it. It didn't have a cat. Flap and I heard about the cat only yesterday. We forgot to tell the others."

"Cad tá sibh á rá?" arsa Arán.

When he heard about the new cat at the new supermarket, he said, "Agus anois, tá ar na lucha misniúla sin a mbeatha a chur i mbaol chun fáilte a chur romhainne."

Flap burst into tears when she heard this. "Arán says that those three brave mice have put their lives in danger just to welcome himself and Michael." She gave a great moan. "And oh 'tis true, 'tis true," she said.

"And I am to blame," Michael said. "I am to blame. It was I who first spoke of the cake."

"Ach cad táimid ag dhéanamh annseo?" arsa Arán. He picked his stick up off the ground. "Amach linn ón seomra seo. Síos go dtí an siopa linn go léir."

All the others knew without being told what Arán had said.

It was in the supermarket they ought to be, and not talking in the drawingroom.

Down the stairs they ran.

Arán looked like a general leading a charge.

So did Michael for he too held his walking stick above his head.

As they rushed out into the bright sunlight they ran head first into old Crumbs who was just coming in from the garden.

"Ah, ha, ah, ha," smirked old Crumbs. "In too much of a hurry to even look where you are going. I always knew the Matchless Mice would get what they deserved."

The four Matchless Mice stared at old Crumbs in amazement. Then suddenly Flap stopped shivering and

crying. She became as cold as ice.

When she spoke her voice sounded like the North Wind.

"Old Crumbs Kitchen," she said. "I know that you and Grandfather Matchless have not been the best of friends. I know too," she said, "that Grandfather can get on other mice's nerves. But what I did not know was that there would ever be a mouse as wicked as you are. You have deliberately allowed Grandfather Matchless to lead himself and Grandmother and our own little Scratch into danger. If anything happens to them, it will be your fault."

Then she turned to the others. "Come along quickly," she said. "We have wasted enough time as it is."

Off they ran down the drive and out of sight.

Old Crumbs was stunned. He had never for one moment thought that any real harm would come to Grandfather or Grandmother Matchless or to little Scratch.

Little Scratch was the nicest little mouse in the Mansion.

If anything happened to little Scratch, no mouse in the Mansion would ever talk to old Crumbs again.

There was only one thing that old Crumbs could do now.

He would have to go after the others.

He would have to try and help.

Oh if only it was not too late!

Old Crumbs ran down the steps and off as fast as his poor old legs would carry him, across the garden.

In a few minutes he was standing at the great rusting gates of Mangold Mansion, staring out at the great world beyond.

8

The Supermarket

Little Scratch ran along beside Grandfather and Grandmother Matchless.

For two such old mice, Grandfather and Grandmother Matchless could run very fast indeed.

Little Scratch did not find it very easy at all to keep up with them. Also he did not care very much for the endless line of huge lorries and trucks and cars that rushed by.

It was his first time away from the Mansion. The outside world seemed to be a noisy, nasty, dangerous place.

Little Scratch said to himself, "Michael and Arán must be very brave mice to have come such long distances to see us. I wonder will I ever be brave enough to go on a long journey all by myself."

Grandfather Matchless stopped and pointed at a great glass building on the other side of the road. "That," he said, "is the supermarket."

"But what about the traffic?" little Scratch asked. "How are we going to cross the road without getting run over?"

"We will use the gutter and drain route," said Grandfather. "There is one grating here. Therefore there must be another over there."

"Oh dear, must we?" asked Grandmother, "You know how nervous travelling underground makes me."

"Only take a flash," said Grandfather. "And with this

fine weather, there will be no risk of flooding."

Grandfather dropped down through the grating. Grandmother closed her eyes tightly and followed him.

Then came little Scratch.

The drain was like a long black tunnel with just a

faint slit of light way, way at the other end.

Grandfather pointed at this slit of light, "There's the other grating," he said. "I knew I was right."

He was right too about there being no flooding. The drain was as dry as a bone.

It also had a very interesting collection of things left there from the last rainy day. There were empty matchboxes, sweet papers, several pieces of orange peel and a large piece of cardboard with a drawing of a chicken on it.

"Hurry, Scratch, hurry," Grandmother said.

Little Scratch stopped looking around him and hurried off after Grandmother and Grandfather.

The drain was darkest in the middle where there was a second larger drain that carried away the rain water. There was no sign of light anywhere inside it.

From the quick glance he had of it, the large drain looked like the most mysterious place he had ever seen.

"It would be lovely to come back and really explore," Scratch thought.

Then he realised that he was having an adventure.

"An adventure," he said out loud. The sound of his voice echoed around the drain.

"An adventure, an adventure," he said the word again.

"Please, Scratch, you must keep up with us," Grandmother Matchless called back to him.

She and Grandfather were already standing under the other grating.

The sunlight which streamed down on them seemed much, much brighter after the darkness of the drain.

All three mice blinked.

"Now when we get outside," Grandfather said, "we must move as quickly as we can in single file. Keep close to the wall. That way we will not be seen."

Once more Grandfather led the way.

Then came Grandmother.

Then came little Scratch.

They followed the wall around the car park. It led them straight to the door of the supermarket.

Together they looked in through the glass door. The place looked empty. There was just row upon row upon row of shelves of all kinds of food.

Little Scratch had never seen so much food in his life.

In fact little Scratch has never even IMAGINED there could be so much food in the whole world.

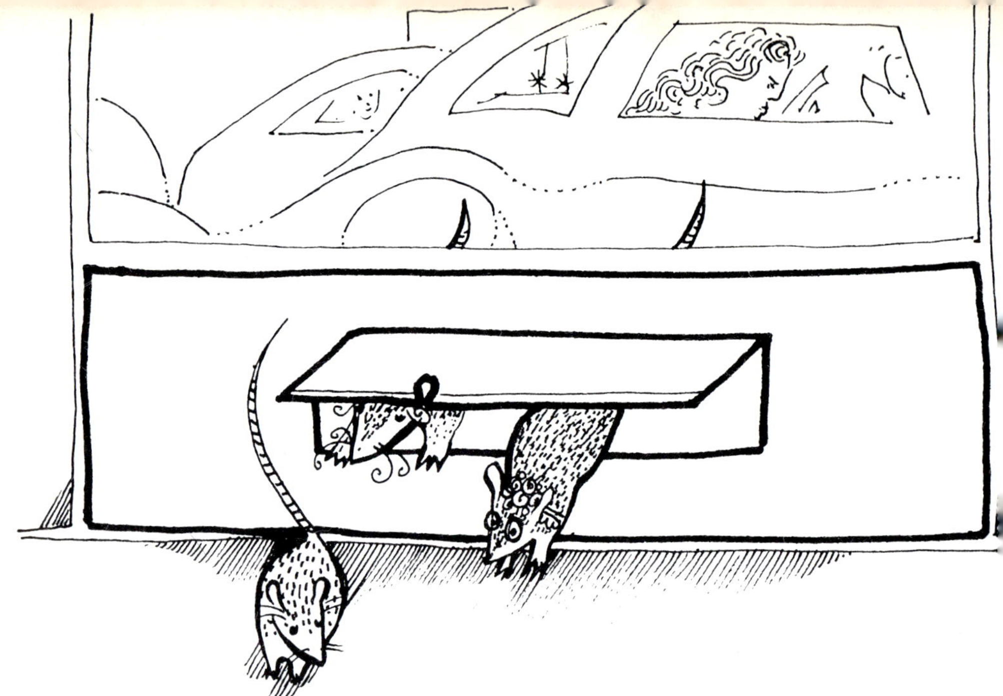

"Letter box," said Grandfather.

The letter box opened very easily.

The three mice slipped in through it and landed on the door mat.

Grandfather glanced quickly around. "We'll need something to carry the cake ingredients back to Mangold Mansion."

"The inside of a match box would be perfect," Grandmother said.

"I can find that," little Scratch said.

"Alright," said Grandfather. "Grandmother and I will go out to the store room. That's always the best place to start looking for stuff. Humans can be so careless. They leave so much lying around."

"Don't go wandering off," Grandmother warned little Scratch. "In a place this size, you could easily get lost."

She looked unhappily around her. "I liked this place much better when it was just a shop," she said.

9

The Cat

Meanwhile Arán and Michael and Moaner and Flap had run so fast that they were now across the road from the supermarket.

In fact they were standing on exactly the same spot as little Scratch and his grandparents had stood.

But none of them thought of using the drain to cross the road. Instead they had to just stand there and wait for a break in the traffic.

Michael, in spite of being so worried, was glad to rest for even a few seconds. Living in Manchester he didn't get very much exercise. In fact he had not had so much exercise in years. He was out of breath.

Suddenly the road was clear. Two huge lorries had made all the other traffic slow down behind them.

Moaner and the others dashed across the road into the car park.

"Just a second," Michael said. "Plan of action."

"What?" said Moaner.

"Plan of action," Michael said. "Terribly sorry, out of breath. No good will come of just blundering into the shop."

Ach bhí Arán ag féachaint go haireach ar an siopa.

Michael noticed the expression on Arán's face. "Why is Arán staring so carefully at the shop?" he asked. "Maybe HE has a plan of action."

"Creidim go bhfuil an siopa dúnta," arsa Arán.

"B'fhéidir gur lá saoire atá ann."

"Tá an ceart agat," arsa Flap. She turned to the others. "Arán thinks the shop is closed, that it must be half-day."

There were no cars in the car park.

But no sooner had she spoken than Arán gave a little jump. "Tá Scratch agus an Seanathair agus an Seanmháthair ag rith thar an fhuinneog," ar seisean.

"Then they are safe, safe," Flap said. "Arán says he just saw the three of them run by the window."

"Inside or out?" asked Moaner.

"Inside of course," said Flap. "But what difference does that make?"

"Because inside, without any people, means they are inside by themselves with the cat," Moaner said grimly.

Flap flung herself forward. Calling out at the top of her voice, she ran towards the supermarket. "Scratch, Scratch, Scratch," she yelled. "Grandfather, Grandmother . . . Beware . . . Beware."

In her hurry, she did not realise that the supermarket was made of glass.

She ran straight into one of the walls and gave herself such a bang! that she fell head over heels onto the ground.

"What happened?" she asked. "Not secret weapons? Surely not secret weapons?"

"No, no nothing like that at all," said Moaner. He bent down to lift her up. Then he became like a statue and dropped her again, "Oh breadcrumbs and vinegar," he said. "Breadcrumbs and vinegar."

Flap scrambled to her feet. She looked in the same direction as Moaner.

At first she saw only little Scratch. He was coming around the side of a counter. He was dragging the inside of a matchbox behind him. "That must be for the shopping," said Flap.

Moaner stretched out a quivering paw.

Flap looked towards the top of the counter.

What she saw almost made her fall back down onto the ground again.

There on top of the counter, gazing down on little Scratch, was the biggest cat Flap had ever seen!

It had a long, long tail with a black tip to it!

The tail kept twitching very slowly back and forth!

"Scratch! Scratch!" screamed Flap.

Once more she flung herself against the glass wall! She pounded on it with her fists. Again and again she called "Scratch! Scratch!"

But the glass was too thick. Little Scratch could not hear his mother.

Then something made little Scratch look around him. He had the feeling he was being watched.

In fact he was sure he was being watched!

Then to his surprise, he saw Arán and Michael and Moaner and Flap all staring in at him!

They must have come to help with the shopping. But why did they look so odd! Why were their eyes like glass? Why was Flap banging like that on the window? She seemed to be trying to say something.

"Of course, I know what it is," Scratch said to himself. "They want to know how to get into the supermarket."

"Letter box," he shouted. "Use the letterbox."

But none of them moved.

He shouted even louder. "Letter box. Use the letter box."

Grandfather and Grandmother Matchless came running out of the store room.

"What's all this racket?" Grandfather demanded . . . Then his eyes went all glassy, just like the mice outside.

So did Grandmother's.

"Don't move," said Grandfather without opening his mouth.

"What do you mean, Grandfather?" asked little Scratch.

"Don't move, that's all. Don't move."

"Is it a new game, like statues?" little Scratch asked. It seemed a very strange time for games.

Then out of the corner of his eye, he saw something black move.

He turned his head.

The black thing looked like the end of a tail.

It was a tail.

But the tail of what?

Suddenly little Scratch knew. It was the tail of a cat. The monster on top of the counter was a CAT!

And the cat was ready to jump on him.

The cat moved about half an inch.

Its shadow fell over little Scratch.

Little Scratch closed his eyes. He was terrified.

Then suddenly there was the loud crash of the flap of the letter box. Onto the door mat tumbled Michael, Arán, Moaner and Flap. They had at last guessed what Scratch had been shouting at them.

"Stand back from that young mouse," shouted Michael, "or, by gum, I'll fix you."

Arán shook his stick angrily. "Brisfidh mé do cheann," ar seisean. "Is le Arán MacLeasa ón Lios in aice leis an Sliabh Mór atá tú ag caint anois."

Then the most extraordinary thing happened! Instead of springing forward to attack the mice, the cat said, in the most afraid kind of voice, "Ph . . please, please, don't touch me! Don't touch me! I am in such a state of nerves being locked in here by myself."

"Well, I declare to the blue-cheese moon," declared Grandfather. "Who ever heard of a cat being afraid of a mouse?"

"Oh it's not just mice," said the cat. "Or at least, I

mean. I am trying to say . . . I wasn't going to touch this little mouse here. I was going to ask if I could help."

Grandmother at once asked the cat to fill the match box with the ingredients for the cake.

All the time the cat kept trembling.

Flap couldn't help feeling sorry for him. "After all," she thought, "it's bad enough to be a cat, without being afraid as well."

"What's your name, Cat?" she asked.

"It's Fred Faraway," said the cat. "But most other cats call me 'Frightened Fred'."

"But we were told that the cat in this supermarket was very fierce," said Moaner.

"Oh you must be thinking of the cat who was here before me. He was known as 'The Terrible Miaow'. He's been given one of the finest jobs a cat can have. He's guarding a fish shop. All I want from life is to be left alone," said Fred.

"Well we won't hurt you," little Scratch said.

By now the matchbox was full. It was time to go back to the Mansion.

Fred, the cat, very kindly held the flap of the letter-box open. The mice lowered the matchbox to the ground.

"Good-bye and thank you," said Flap. "If you are ever near to Mangold Mansion, come and see us."

It was at that moment that old Crumbs arrived in the car park. He had lost his way several times. He had almost been run over by a lorry. A nasty dog had chased him up a drain-pipe. But still he had gone on in the hope of saving little Scratch.

Now what did he see at the end of all his trouble?

He saw the so-called terrible cat HELPING the mice get a matchbox through the letterbox of the supermarket.

What did he hear?

He heard Flap, who had called him 'wicked', actually inviting the cat to come and visit.

"So I was right all along," he said to himself. "The Matchless Mice are up to more tricks. They will pretend to be brave because they went to the supermarket. All the time they were friends with the cat."

And what would the other mice say when they heard that the Matchless Mice were friends with a CAT?

Old Crumbs hid around a corner.

He watched the Matchless Mice carry off their matchbox of shopping.

He saw them go down through the grating in the gutter.

A few minutes later, he saw them come up safely through the gutter on the other side of the road.

Old Crumbs said, "They think by baking a cake that all will be forgotten and forgiven. Well, it won't."

He started to run across the car park.

He glanced at the door of the supermarket. There, looking sadly out at him, was Fred the Cat.

But whoever heard of a sad cat? old Crumbs asked himself.

Yet Fred was sad. He had liked the Matchless Mice. But who was this other mouse outside now, looking at him?

There was something strange about that mouse.

Something that made Fred feel that the Matchless Mice might be in trouble.

10

The Matchless Mice bake a Cake

When the Matchless Mice arrived back at Mangold Mansion, dozens of mice rushed out to meet them.

"Where have you been?"

"What have you got in the box?"

The Matchless Mice were asked dozens of questions.

But all Grandfather would say was, "We've just been shopping. We went down as far as the supermarket."

"The supermarket!" screamed Alta Attica. "But the cat? What about the fierce cat?"

"No problem," said Grandfather Matchless. "Between us we took care of the cat. Now if you will excuse us we have to bake a cake. When it's ready, you are all welcome to help us eat it. You can meet our visitors then as well."

Alta Attic and all the other mice stared open-mouthed as Grandfather Matchless led the rest of the Matchless Mice up the front steps.

"Well, there is a brave mouse," said Alta.

"Brave is as brave does," said Polly Pantry. "I've a feeling in my bones that there is more to this than meets the eye."

"Don't be silly," said Alta Attic. "If there was, old Crumbs would be here to tell us. We should never have listened to old Crumbs in the first place. Grandfather Matchless is terrific!"

Alta Attic always spoke in a very loud voice. This was

because she lived right at the top of the house. Grandfather Matchless had no trouble hearing what she had just said about him now. He was delighted. So were Scratch and Arán and Michael and Moaner and Flap and Grandmother.

But, in spite of being so pleased, Grandmother was also feeling very serious.

As soon as they were in the drawingroom, Grandmother said to Grandfather. "It might be a good idea to talk to Arán. We need to know the full story of the Matchless Mice. Not just for our sake, but for the sake of little Scratch as well."

"Very well," said Grandfather. "I'll find out all I can. But first we'd better get on with making the cake."

Grandfather Matchless and Moaner lit a tiny fire in the corner of the huge drawingroom fireplace.

Grandmother and Flap set to work, mixing the cake.

Soon the room was filled with the most delicious smell of cooking.

"Now everyone get comfortable," Grandmother said. "Scratch and Michael stay by the door. Keep watch for any mice listening. Keep watch especially for old Crumbs."

"Strange he wasn't here when we got back," Moaner said.

"If I never see him again, I won't cry," declared Grandfather. "Now Flap, are you ready to translate all that Arán has to say?"

"I am of course," said Flap.

Arán began to speak very slowly so that Flap could understand him.

Then, when he had finished one piece, he would stop.

Flap would then tell the others in English what had been said.

It went like this.

Arán said, "Fadó, fadó, cúpla bliain sul ar rugadh mise, bhí ár gclann inár gcónaí sa lios mór in aice an Sliabh Mór."

Flap said in English, "Long, long ago, a few years before even I was born, our family lived in the great fort near the big Mountain."

Arán said, 'Ní raibh aon rud ag cur isteach orainn!"

Flap said, "We were as contented as could be."

Arán said, "Bhí ár ndóthain le h-ithe againn. Bhí ár ndóthain le h-ól.

"We had plenty to eat and plenty to drink."

"Bhíomar inár gcónaí sa Lios timpeall cuig chéad bliain. Sin é an chúis gur tugadh an tainm MacLeasa orainn."

"We had been living in the Fort for almost five hundred years. That is the reason why we were called the Mac Leasas."

"What, what, what?" spluttered Grandfather, when he heard this. "I don't follow that. What does he mean that the family was called 'Macleasa' because they'd lived in the fort for so long?"

"It means 'the son of the Fort'," said Flap, "or the family that have lived longest in the fort. It's like in English when sometimes towns are named after people. Or people are named after towns."

"Anglicised," said little Scratch.

"Stop that," said Grandfather. He thought little Scratch was using bad language..

"Little Scratch is right," said Flap. "That's the right word – anglicised. It's when a word gets changed into English. There is a human name – O'Sullivan. In Irish, the name is O'Súileabhaín – the son of the man with one eye."

"And our name MacLeasa became Matchless," Grandmother said.

"Well, anyway let's get on with the story," Grandfather said crossly. He was beginning to feel nervous about what else Arán might have to say.

Arán stared silently at Grandfather. Then he said to Flap. "Ní thuigim cé'n fáth nach bhfuil an scéal seo agaibh go léir fós."

"Oh bhí saghas scéil againn," arsa Flap.

"Saghas scéil!" arsa Arán. "Cé'n rud é, 'saghas scéil'? Níl ach aon scéal amáin ann. Sin an scéal ceart!"

"Oh tá an ceart agat," arsa Flap. "Ach bhí athair Grandfather an-mhóralách ar fad."

"Agus an bhfuil tú ag rá go raibh cúis éigin aige náire a beith air faoina chlann?" arsa Arán.

"Oh níl mé ag rá so in aonchor," said Flap.

Grandfather banged the floor with his foot. "Are you forgetting you are supposed to be explaining every word Arán is saying?" he shouted at Flap.

"Oh I'm sorry," said Flap. "I was just explaining to Arán about how proud your father was."

"Well never mind explaining anything to him," said Grandfather. "HE is supposed to be explaining to us. So far all we know is that he comes from a well-off family that lived in a fort and they had no worries. Ask him what this trouble, 'an trioblóid' was that my father was in . . ."

The story Arán told them was simple and sad.

Grandfather's father's real name was Ím.

Arán's father's name was Ubh.

They had been the very best of friends.

Then one day there had been a great quarrel over a dried chestnut.

Ím and Ubh had both found the chestnut at the same moment.

Ubh said it belonged to him.

Ím said it belonged to him.

The quarrel had become so bad that it was decided that Ubh being the oldest should keep the dried chestnut.

Im thought this was very unfair. Without a word to anyone, he had walked out of the Fort. He had never come back. It was only by chance that the Mac Leasas had learned that he had gone to live in Mangold Mansion.

"And what sort of mice were they to treat my father like that?" Grandfather demanded. "Ask Arán that."

"Na lucha is fearr ar domhan, cróga, galánta, cliste," b'shin an freagra a fuair siad ó Arán.

"Arán says they were the bravest, most gallant, most clever mice in the world." That was the answer Arán gave them.

"Yet they let my father go off into the world by himself." Then he stopped as a name came into his mind. "Ashes," he said, "Ashes."

"Oh dear," said Flap, thinking Grandfather was sneezing. "I hope you haven't caught a cold."

It was Grandmother who answered. Her eyes filled with tears as she spoke. "No, it's not a cold," she said. "He is remembering how he sent his own brother away from here. Ashes was Michael's father."

"I never heard about my father being sent away," declared Michael.

"Well, it was over something more serious than a

dried chestnut," said Grandfather. "All the same, I wish now that I hadn't."

"Ba mhaith liom an scéal a chríochnú," arsa Arán.

"Arán would like to finish his story," said Flap.

The other mice listened carefully.

"Na rudai a thárla idir t'athair agus m'athair, tá síad thart anois."

"The things that happened between my father and yours are in the past now," Arán said to Grandfather.

"Tá fáilte roimh gach aoinne agaibh teacht ar ais to dtí an Lios liom."

"Any of you are welcome to come back to the Fort with me."

"Well that's good of you," said Grandfather.

"The same goes from me and my Dad," said Michael. "My Dad doesn't blame you for anything that's happened. He's doing very well in Manchester."

"And the most important thing is still true," declared Grandfather. "The Matchless Mice did get their name because they lived longer than any other mouse family in the same place. We just happen to be the Mangold Mansion branch of the family."

Things were going so well that little Scratch felt like giving three loud cheers.

Then he heard a sound on the stairs. It was old Crumbs, back at last from the supermarket.

He ran to the drawingroom door.

"Hey, hey," said Michael. "You can't go in there."

"Oh and you'll stop me, I suppose?" snapped old Crumbs.

"I'm sorry," said Scratch, "but Uncle Michael is right . . ."

Old Crumbs stared at Scratch. "What did you call this razzle-dazzle streak of hair-oil here beside you?"

"He's my Uncle Michael from Manchester," said Scratch.

"Well, yes, I suppose I am," said Michael grinning happily. "You are a very clever little mouse to know that."

Suddenly there was a sound of voices down at the front door. Human voices!

"Humans" whispered Michael. "Quick inside."

Scratch, Michael and old Crumbs ran into the drawingroom.

"Humans," said Michael. "Down in the hall."

"Oh dear," said Grandmother. "What could have brought humans here?"

"The Matchless Mice did," said old Crumbs. "Mice who light fires attract humans."

"They are coming upstairs," Flap shrieked. "What'll we do?"

"Get rid of them," said Michael.

He beckoned to Arán. Together they ran into the middle of the room.

Slowly two women came into the room.

At first they didn't see the mice.

They stared instead at the fireplace.

"You're right," said one of the women. "There is a fire here. But it's so small."

At that moment, Michael and Arán both gave loud yells.

The women stared at them in horror. Then slowly, very slowly, they began to back away.

"Mice," gasped the first woman.

"Dressed in clothes," whispered the second.

"Belinda, are we seeing things, " whispered the first.

"I don't know and I don't care. I'd always heard this place was haunted. I'm getting out of here."

The two women ran out of the room, down the stairs and away across the garden out of sight.

Michael and Arán laughed and shook paws.

"Ni tiocfaidh siad ar ais arís," arsa Arán.

"If he has said what I think he has said, then Arán is right," said Michael. "That's the last human we will see here for a while."

"Tricks," shouted old Crumbs, "Tricks. More tricks. Well, I'll show you!"

The Matchless Mice all stared at each other.

"What does he mean by 'tricks'?" Michael asked.

"I don't know but I think we'd better see what he is up to. Come on," said Grandfather.

The Matchless Mice rushed out of the drawingroom and down the stairs after old Crumbs.

11

Fred joins the Party

Old Crumbs, in fact, had no idea of where he was going or what he was going to do.

He was in a terrible temper. Everything he had tried to do had gone wrong. Even when he had tried to help save little Scratch, he had been too late.

Now the Matchless Mice seemed to be on top of the world.

He'd met Alta Attic before going into the house. She had pointed at him and said, "Silly old Crumbs. Go back to the kitchen where you belong."

Even Polly Pantry had not seemed so friendly. "Oh, hello, Crumbs," she had said, "Where have you been?"

Then she hurried off without even waiting for an answer.

It was enough to drive a mouse right away from Mangold Mansion.

"They just don't behave the way mice should," old Crumbs said to himself. "They make friends with cats. They probably even knew those two humans. It is all a trick to try and fool us. If only I could think of a really good way to show them up."

Then he heard a strange noise.

It was the sound of mice yelling.

Out of the long grass came Polly Pantry.

Behind her was Alta Attic.

Then came ten or twelve other mice.

They were all screaming.

"Silly mice," old Crumbs shouted at them. "What did you see? A couple of humans? They are friends of the Matchless Mice."

"Not humans," gasped Polly Parlour. "A cat, a monster cat."

"More of the Matchless Mice's tricks," said old Crumbs. "The cat is a friend of theirs."

"Are you mad?" cried Alta Attic.

"They invited the cat here," said old Crumbs. "Where is the cat?"

"Over there," said Alta Attic. "It's prowling around the oak tree."

"Watch this then," said old Crumbs.

Before any mouse could stop him, old Crumbs ran down the front steps. He stopped at the edge of the long grass.

"Hey you," he shouted. "Hey, Pussy Cat, come to see your friends, have you?"

The long grass was parted by a very large paw. A pair of bright green eyes stared down at old Crumbs.

"You'll find the Matchless Mice in the drawingroom, baking a cake," old Crumbs said. "Come on. I'll show you the way."

Old Crumbs turned back to the Mansion just as the Matchless Mice came running out.

"There they are," old Crumbs shouted. "There are your friends."

He waved to the Matchless Mice. "Why don't you come and say hello to your friend from the supermarket?"

"Because that is not the supermarket cat," Grandfather yelled back.

All the other mice gave a gasp of horror and moved back a few paces.

Old Crumbs gave a short laugh. "Not the cat from the supermarket?" he said. "Funny, very funny, I don't think."

Then a terrible thought occurred to him. The cat in the grass behind him was a dirty yellow colour.

The cat he had seen at the supermarket had been orange with a black tip to its tail.

Old Crumbs looked over his shoulder.

The cat was still there.

"Go away," old Crumbs said suddenly. "Clear off."

The cat stared at him in surprise. Then a deep fierce growl began way down in its throat.

It arched its back. It got ready to spring forward.

Then suddenly there was a flash of orange fur.

The yellow cat was knocked back into the long grass.

"It's Fred," yelled little Scratch. "It's Fred."

And indeed it was Fred, the cat from the supermarket.

Fred gave the yellow cat another thump with his paw. "These mice are friends of mine," he said. "Leave them alone."

The yellow cat scrambled away through the long grass. "We will see about that," it said. "I'll go and tell the Tough Cat Gang what you just did."

"Tell who you like," said Fred. "Just don't come back here."

The yellow cat ran out of sight.

"Oh Fred, how brave you were," said little Scratch. "No one will ever be able to call you 'Frightened Fred' again."

"Well, when I saw old Crumbs down at the supermarket, I felt something might be wrong," said Fred. "That's why I came up here."

"And a very good thing you did too," said Grandmother Matchless. "Now the cake should be ready so why don't we all go up into the drawingroom and eat it?"

"I like the look of this place," said Fred. "I might stay."

"Oh do, do," said little Scratch. "It would be great to have a cat to protect us."

And so all the mice were happy, all except old Crumbs that is.

He stayed out in the hall. He listened to the sound of the party in the drawingroom. He looked at the faint trickle of smoke from the fireplace.

"Those humans will come back," he said. "And as for Fred living here? Cats and mice never mix. The Matchless Mice may think they have won the day. But they haven't. There will be more trouble at Mangold Mansion."

And was old Crumbs right?

Well, that's another story.

Dedicated
with affection to
Rosaleen Linehan
who first read
The Matchless Mice
on RTE's
Storyroom

"Now, who ever heard of a dedication at the back of a book," said old Crumbs Kitchen, disagreeable to the last.
"But, this isn't the end," said Scratch, "This is the BEGINNING of the further adventures of the Matchless Mice. There'll be lots and lots of books all about us."
"Rubbish," snapped old Crumbs, "Who'd want to read . . ." but before he could finish, little Scratch was already running off to the next big adventure. Watch out!